About Skill Builders Math

by Jeanne S. Rawlins

Welcome to RBP Books' Skill Builders series. Like our Summer Bridge Activities collection, the Skill Builders series is designed to make learning both fun and rewarding.

Skill Builders 6th Grade Math provides students with focused practice to help them reinforce and develop math skills. Each Skill Builders volume is grade-level appropriate, with clear examples and instructions to guide the lesson. In accordance with NCTM standards, exercises for grade six cover a variety of math skills, including multidigit addition, subtraction, multiplication, and division; word problems; life skills; graphing; geometry; exponents; introductory algebra; ratios; fractions, decimals, and percents.

A critical thinking section includes exercises to develop higher order thinking skills.

Learning is more effective when approached with an element of fun and enthusiasm—just as most children approach life. That's why the Skill Builders combine entertaining and academically sound exercises and fun themes to make reviewing basic skills fun and effective, for both you and your budding scholars.

Table of Contents

Addition

Solve each problem below.

1. 68 + 47	**2.** 46 + 59	**3.** 586 + 73	**4.** 857 + 48	**5.** 842 + 734

6. 4,931 + 3,562	**7.** 6,328 + 2,325	**8.** 2,179 + 891	**9.** 8,478 + 2,950

10. 358 + 80 =   **11.** 875 + 20 =   **12.** 786 + 321 =

13. 4,387 + 421 =   **14.** 7,643 + 416 =

15. 2,582 + 1,809 =   **16.** 3,719 + 1,427 =

Addition

Solve each problem below.

1. 468
    + 246

2. 2,486
    + 2,274

3. 12,484
    + 8,392

4. 6,472
    + 2,428

5. 38,926
    + 6,008

6. 54,789
    + 19,740

7. 45,489
    + 28,254

8. 7,367
    + 2,945

9.   67
     42
    + 74

10. 439
     214
    + 894

11. 4,832
     3,423
    + 7,890

12. 3,219
     7,225
    + 3,545

13. 3,721 + 2,630 =

14. 2,793 + 4,199 =

15. 5,731 + 344 + 98 =

16. 665 + 482 + 988 =

Subtraction

Solve each problem below.

1.   83
        − 26

2.   64
        − 19

3. 962
        − 46

4. 387
        − 29

5. 542
        − 139

6. 468
        − 273

7. 531
        − 103

8. 3,268
        − 825

9. 7,834
        − 497

10. $56 - 29 =$

11. $827 - 342 =$

12. $76 - 29 =$

13. $4,656 - 941 =$

14. $5,247 - 3,217 =$

15. $6,148 - 3,463 =$

16. $5,943 - 3,694 =$

Math Grade 6—RBP0059

Subtraction

Solve each problem below.

1. 708
  − 439

2. 500
  − 217

3. 600
  − 250

4. 550
  − 91

5. 286
  − 127

6. 306
  − 107

7. 5,060
  − 3,862

8. 5,000
  − 3,802

9. 6,258
  − 3,269

10. 9,206
  − 2,846

11. 13,800
  − 3,096

12. 80,060
  − 26,124

13. 8,723
  − 3,942

14. 301 − 280 =

15. 6,004 − 831 =

16. 596 − 97 =

17. 7,600 − 5,423 =

18. 70,060 − 2,083 =

Multiplication

Solve each problem below.

1. 8
x 3

2. 6
x 4

3. 9
x 5

4. 10
x 7

5. 7
x 2

6. 8
x 7

7. 16
x 3

8. 34
x 4

9. 22
x 6

10. 42
x 7

11. 64
x 9

12. 42 • 3 =

13. 64 • 5 =

14. 91 • 8 =

15. 146
x 8

16. 467
x 3

17. 286
x 7

18. 876
x 2

19. 443
x 4

20. 893 • 6 =

21. 930 • 5 =

22. 813 • 3 =

23. 46
x 22

24. 98
x 30

25. 67
x 42

26. 59
x 34

Multiplication

Solve each problem.

1. 2,473
   x   3

2. 6,518
   x   6

3. 9,436
   x   4

4. 203
   x 15

5. 729
   x 21

6. 432
   x 34

7. 385
   x 43

Figure the cost of the following:

8. 2 pepperoni pizzas _____

9. 4 Hawaiian pizzas _____

10. 3 cheese pizzas_____

11. 1 cheese, 1 pepperoni,

and 1 sausage pizza _____

12. 2 Hawaiian and

1 pepperoni pizza_____

Paul's Pizza	
Cheese	$ 7.99
Pepperoni	$ 8.99
Sausage............	$ 9.49
Hawaiian	$ 9.99

Mental Math and Magic Squares

Can you do these problems in your head?

1. 2 x 10 =

2. 9 x 10 =

3. 5 x 60 =

4. 33 x 10 =

5. 6 x 40 =

6. 15 x 10 =

7. 8 x 30 =

8. 50 x 5 =

9. 24 x 10 =

10. 9 x 60 =

11. 50 x 8 =

12. 5 x 20 =

Magic Squares

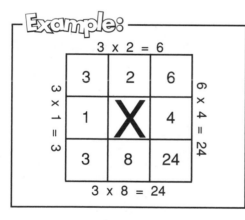

Example:

3 x 2 = 6

3 x 1 = 3

6 x 4 = 24

3 x 8 = 24

3	2	6
1	X	4
3	8	24

13.

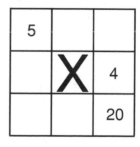

5		
	X	4
		20

14.

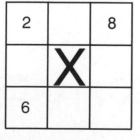

2		8
	X	
6		

15.

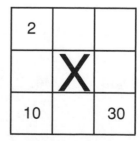

2		
	X	
10		30

Division

Solve each problem.

1. $16 \div 2 =$

2. $24 \div 6 =$

3. $27 \div 3 =$

4. $30 \div 5 =$

5. $5\overline{)30}$

6. $4\overline{)12}$

7. $8\overline{)56}$

8. $7\overline{)28}$

9. $2\overline{)0}$

10. $9\overline{)36}$

11. $1\overline{)7}$

12. $8\overline{)32}$

13. $5\overline{)95}$

14. $3\overline{)42}$

15. $6\overline{)90}$

16. $6\overline{)84}$

17. $2\overline{)94}$

18. $9\overline{)81}$

19. $6\overline{)78}$

20. $5\overline{)100}$

21. $6\overline{)498}$

22. $4\overline{)388}$

23. $8\overline{)560}$

24. $3\overline{)1968}$

25. $6\overline{)2142}$

Division with a Remainder

Solve the following problems.

1. $2\overline{)7}$

2. $5\overline{)21}$

3. $4\overline{)9}$

4. $6\overline{)39}$

5. $17 \div 3 =$

6. $19 \div 9 =$

7. $22 \div 8 =$

8. $64 \div 10 =$

9. $7\overline{)44}$

10. $3\overline{)25}$

11. $2\overline{)15}$

12. $5\overline{)33}$

13. $3\overline{)55}$

14. $2\overline{)61}$

15. $9\overline{)29}$

16. $6\overline{)87}$

Math Grade 6—RBP0059

Division with a Remainder

Solve each problem below.

1. $94 \div 5 =$ **2.** $74 \div 4 =$ **3.** $46 \div 7 =$ **4.** $61 \div 5 =$

5. $6 \overline{)843}$ **6.** $4 \overline{)549}$ **7.** $7 \overline{)664}$ **8.** $5 \overline{)842}$

9. $3 \overline{)802}$ **10.** $8 \overline{)521}$ **11.** $9 \overline{)747}$ **12.** $2 \overline{)463}$

13. $683 \div 4 =$ **14.** $549 \div 6 =$ **15.** $429 \div 2 =$ **16.** $843 \div 3 =$

Number of dollar bills	Number of friends	Dollar bills for each friend	Dollar bills left over	Write as an equation
21	4	5	1	$4)\overline{21}$ 5 R1 20 1
8	3			
10	5			
13	2			
18	6			
14	4			
26	7			
32	9			
27	5			

Equivalent Fractions

If you multiply the numerator and denominator by the same number or divide the numerator and denominator by the same number, you have a fraction equal or equivalent to the original fraction.

Example:

$$\frac{1}{2} = \frac{4}{8} \qquad\qquad \frac{1 \times 4}{2 \times 4} = \frac{4}{8} \qquad\qquad \frac{4 \div 4}{8 \div 4} = \frac{1}{2}$$

Rename the following:

1. $\frac{1}{3} = \frac{}{9}$ **2.** $\frac{4}{5} = \frac{}{20}$ **3.** $\frac{3}{4} = \frac{}{12}$ **4.** $\frac{5}{6} = \frac{}{18}$

5. $\frac{2}{3} =$ $\dfrac{}{6}$ $\dfrac{}{9}$ $\dfrac{}{12}$ $\dfrac{}{15}$ $\dfrac{}{18}$ $\dfrac{}{21}$ $\dfrac{}{24}$

6. $\frac{3}{5} =$ $\dfrac{}{10}$ $\dfrac{}{15}$ $\dfrac{}{20}$ $\dfrac{}{25}$ $\dfrac{}{30}$ $\dfrac{}{35}$ $\dfrac{}{40}$

7. $\frac{1}{2} =$ **8.** $\frac{3}{8} =$ **9.** $\frac{1}{12} =$ **10.** $\frac{4}{7} =$

11. $\frac{4}{5} =$ **12.** $\frac{2}{3} =$ **13.** $\frac{5}{10} =$ **14.** $\frac{6}{12} =$

Least Common Multiple (LCM)

Find multiples of the following:

2 = 4, 6, 8, 10, 12, ___, 16, ___, ___, 22, ___, ___

3 = 6, 9, ___, 15, ___, ___, 24, ___, 30, ___, 36, ___

4 = 8, ___, 16, ___, ___, 28, 32, ___, ___, 44, ___

5 = 10, ___, ___, ___, 30, ___, 40, ___, 50, ___, ___

Finding the Least Common Multiple

The least common multiple is the lowest number that a group of numbers can each divide into evenly.

Example:

9   12

Find the smallest factors of the numbers.

9 = 3 x 3   12 = 3 x 2 x 2

Cross off one of any duplicate common factors and multiply the rest of the numbers.

LCM of 9 and 12 = 3 x 3 x 2 x 2

LCM of 9 and 12 = 36

Write the least common multiple for the following:

1. 2, 3   **2.** 5, 10   **3.** 3, 4   **4.** 3, 5

5. 12, 16   **6.** 5, 8   **7.** 18, 24   **8.** 10, 25

Greatest Common Factor (GCF)

The greatest common factor is the largest number that can divide two numbers with no remainder.

Example:

$$9$$
$$9 = 3 \times 3$$

$$18$$
$$18 = 3 \times 3 \times 2$$

3 x 3 are the common factors so

GCF of 9 and 18 = 3 x 3
GCF of 9 and 18 = 9

Write the greatest common factor for the following:

1. 3, 9   **2.** 10, 30   **3.** 15, 25   **4.** 20, 24

5. 27, 81   **6.** 35, 49   **7.** 54, 90   **8.** 9, 12

9. 15, 30   **10.** 5, 20   **11.** 49, 70   **12.** 20, 100

Mixed Numbers and Improper Fractions

An improper fraction is a fraction where the numerator (top number) is larger than the denominator (bottom number).

To convert an improper fraction into a mixed number, do the following:

First, divide the numerator by the denominator.
Second, place the remainder over the original denominator.

$$\frac{25}{8} \qquad 8\overline{)25} \begin{array}{r} 3\ R1 \\ \hline \\ -24 \\ \hline 1 \end{array} \qquad 3\frac{1}{8}$$

Convert the following improper fractions to mixed numbers:

1. $\frac{8}{3}$ 2. $\frac{16}{5}$ 3. $\frac{23}{5}$ 4. $\frac{39}{10}$

5. $\frac{11}{8}$ 6. $\frac{17}{4}$ 7. $\frac{29}{8}$ 8. $\frac{43}{9}$

9. $\frac{30}{7}$ 10. $\frac{55}{9}$ 11. $\frac{17}{6}$ 12. $\frac{22}{7}$

Math Grade 6—RBP0059

Converting a Mixed Number into an Improper Fraction

$3\frac{1}{4}$

Step 1	Step 2	Step 3
Multiply the whole number and the denominator.	Add the numerator to the answer.	Put the answer over the original denominator.
$3 \times 4 = 12$	$12 + 1 = 13$	$\frac{13}{4}$

Convert the following mixed numbers into improper fractions:

1. $3\frac{1}{4}$

2. $1\frac{1}{5}$

3. $4\frac{2}{5}$

4. $3\frac{4}{5}$

5. $5\frac{3}{7}$

6. $4\frac{2}{9}$

7. $4\frac{1}{8}$

8. $3\frac{2}{5}$

9. $6\frac{2}{3}$

10. $9\frac{3}{4}$

11. $8\frac{1}{2}$

12. $7\frac{6}{7}$

Adding Fractions

Example:

$$\frac{2}{3} + \frac{4}{5} =$$

Step 1
Find a common denominator.

$$\frac{2}{3} \quad \frac{4}{5} \quad \overline{15}$$

Step 2
Change to equivalent fractions.

$2 \times 5 = 10 \qquad 4 \times 3 = 12$
$3 \times 5 = 15 \qquad 5 \times 3 = 15$

Step 3
Add the numerators.

$$\frac{10}{15} + \frac{12}{15} = \frac{22}{15}$$

Step 4
Reduce the answer.

$$\frac{22}{15}$$

$$15\overline{)22} \quad 1\frac{7}{15}$$
$$\underline{-15}$$
$$7$$

Add the following fractions:

1. $\frac{1}{2} + \frac{1}{8} =$ **2.** $\frac{2}{5} + \frac{3}{10} =$ **3.** $\frac{5}{8} + \frac{1}{4} =$

4. $\frac{1}{4} + \frac{1}{8} =$ **5.** $\frac{1}{2} + \frac{3}{4} =$ **6.** $\frac{1}{10} + \frac{4}{5} =$

     Math Grade 6—RBP0059

Fractions

Add the fractions below.

1. $\frac{1}{2} + \frac{1}{10} =$

2. $\frac{4}{8} + \frac{3}{8} =$

3. $\frac{29}{100} + \frac{7}{10} =$

4. $\frac{5}{6} + \frac{1}{3} =$

5. $\frac{2}{3} + \frac{5}{12} =$

6. $\frac{5}{8} + \frac{3}{4} =$

Adding Fractions with Whole Numbers
Add the whole numbers; then add the fractions. Reduce the answer.

Example:

$$4\frac{1}{2} + 3\frac{1}{8} = \qquad 4 + 3 = 7 \qquad 7\frac{5}{8}$$
$$\frac{1}{2} + \frac{1}{8} = \frac{5}{8}$$

Add the following:

7. $4\frac{5}{8} + 1\frac{1}{4} =$

8. $3\frac{3}{4} + 2\frac{5}{8} =$

9. $3\frac{7}{100} + 4\frac{9}{10} =$

10. $1\frac{3}{10} + 2\frac{2}{5} =$

©RBP Books

$$\frac{7}{12} - \frac{1}{3}$$

Step 1	Step 2	Step 3	Step 4
Find a common denominator.	Change to equivalent fractions.	Subtract the numerators.	Reduce the answer.

Step 1
Find a common denominator.

↓

least common multiple of 3 and 12 = 12

Step 2
Change to equivalent fractions.

$\frac{7}{12}$

$\frac{1 \times 4}{3 \times 4} = \frac{4}{12}$

Step 3
Subtract the numerators.

$\frac{7}{12}$
$- \frac{4}{12}$
$\frac{3}{12}$

Step 4
Reduce the answer.

$\frac{3 \div 3}{12 \div 3} = \frac{1}{4}$

Subtract the following fractions:

1. $\frac{7}{12}$ $-\frac{1}{6}$

2. $\frac{8}{9}$ $-\frac{2}{3}$

3. $\frac{4}{5}$ $-\frac{1}{4}$

4. $\frac{1}{2}$ $-\frac{3}{10}$

5. $\frac{3}{4}$ $-\frac{1}{3}$

6. $\frac{1}{2} - \frac{1}{6} =$

7. $\frac{3}{4} - \frac{1}{2} =$

8. $\frac{4}{5} - \frac{1}{10} =$

9. $\frac{5}{6} - \frac{2}{3} =$

10. $\frac{3}{10} - \frac{7}{100} =$

11. $\frac{3}{8} - \frac{5}{16} =$

Subtracting Fractions and Whole Numbers

Put the whole number over 1 and then change it to an equivalent fraction and subtract. Reduce the answer.

Example:

$$4 - \frac{3}{4} =$$

Step 1	Step 2	Step 3	Step 4
Put the whole number over 1.	Change to an equivalent fraction.	Subtract.	Reduce.
$\frac{4}{1} - \frac{3}{4}$	$\frac{4 \times 4}{1 \times 4} = \frac{16}{4} - \frac{3}{4}$	$\frac{16}{4} - \frac{3}{4} = \frac{13}{4}$	$3\frac{1}{4}$

Subtract the following:

1. $5 - \frac{3}{5} =$ **2.** $6 - \frac{1}{4} =$ **3.** $8 - \frac{7}{8} =$ **4.** $4 - \frac{2}{3} =$

5. $8 - \frac{1}{3} =$ **6.** $10 - \frac{1}{2} =$ **7.** $3 - \frac{1}{2} =$ **8.** $5 - \frac{3}{7} =$

9. $2 - \frac{3}{7} =$ **10.** $7 - \frac{4}{9} =$ **11.** $7 - \frac{4}{5} =$ **12.** $8 - \frac{3}{4} =$

Multiplying Fractions

Example:

$$\frac{1}{3} \times \frac{3}{4} =$$

Step 1	Step 2	Step 3
Multiply the numerators.	Multiply the denominators.	Reduce.
$1 \times 3 = 3$	$3 \times 4 = 12$	$\frac{3 \div 3}{12 \div 3} = \frac{1}{4}$

Multiply the fractions and write each answer in simplest form.

1. $\frac{2}{5} \times \frac{1}{4} =$

2. $\frac{1}{4} \times \frac{2}{5} =$

3. $\frac{3}{4} \times \frac{4}{7} =$

4. $\frac{1}{3} \times \frac{3}{6} =$

5. $\frac{5}{8} \times \frac{2}{7} =$

6. $\frac{3}{10} \times \frac{1}{2} =$

7. $\frac{1}{3} \times \frac{3}{7} \times \frac{5}{8} =$

8. $\frac{4}{5} \times \frac{3}{4} \times \frac{2}{3} =$

9. $\frac{9}{10} \times \frac{2}{5} \times \frac{1}{4} =$

10. $\frac{2}{5} \times \frac{1}{8} =$

11. $\frac{4}{10} \times \frac{2}{3} =$

12. $\frac{5}{8} \times \frac{4}{7} =$

13. $\frac{1}{4} \times \frac{2}{6} =$

14. $\frac{2}{5} \times \frac{1}{4} \times \frac{3}{10} =$

15. $\frac{5}{6} \times \frac{3}{4} \times \frac{1}{2} =$

Multiplying Fractions with Whole Numbers

$$3\frac{1}{4} \times 2\frac{2}{3} =$$

Step 1	Step 2	Step 3	Step 4
Convert to improper fractions.	Multiply the numerators.	Multiply the denominators.	Reduce.
$\frac{13}{4} \times \frac{8}{3}$	$13 \times 8 = 104$	$4 \times 3 = 12$	$\frac{104}{12} = 8\frac{8}{12}$ or $8\frac{2}{3}$

Multiply the fractions below, and write each answer as a mixed number.

1. $4\frac{1}{2} \times 2\frac{3}{4} =$ **2.** $3\frac{1}{3} \times 5\frac{3}{10} =$ **3.** $6\frac{2}{5} \times 3\frac{5}{6} =$

4. $7\frac{4}{5} \times 2\frac{9}{10} =$ **5.** $2\frac{1}{4} \times 3\frac{7}{8} =$ **6.** $5\frac{2}{3} \times 1\frac{1}{6} =$

7. $2\frac{3}{4} \times 4\frac{1}{6} =$ **8.** $4\frac{3}{8} \times 6\frac{8}{11} =$ **9.** $4\frac{3}{7} \times 2\frac{4}{9} =$

Dividing Fractions

To divide fractions, invert the second fraction and multiply.

Invert and multiply the following fractions:

1. $\frac{4}{5} \div \frac{2}{3} =$ **2.** $\frac{1}{3} \div \frac{4}{5} =$ **3.** $\frac{2}{5} \div \frac{5}{6} =$

4. $\frac{1}{4} \div \frac{3}{10} =$ **5.** $\frac{5}{8} \div \frac{3}{4} =$ **6.** $\frac{4}{5} \div \frac{1}{2} =$

7. $\frac{2}{9} \div \frac{3}{8} =$ **8.** $\frac{4}{9} \div \frac{1}{5} =$ **9.** $\frac{5}{6} \div \frac{3}{7} =$

10. $\frac{8}{10} \div \frac{4}{5} =$ **11.** $\frac{5}{8} \div \frac{1}{2} =$

Math Grade 6—RBP0059

Adding and Subtracting Decimals

When adding and subtracting decimals, you must line the decimal points up.

Example:

$$3.5 + 1.06 + .45 =$$

Add each column.

```
3.5
1.06
 .45
```

Bring the decimal point straight down.

```
  1 1
  3.5
  1.06
+  .45
  5.01
```

Add the numbers below. Don't forget the decimal point in your answer.

1. $3.63 + 4.8 =$ **2.** $95.02 + 1.15 =$ **3.** $17.7 + 5.2 =$

4. $4.83 + 7.8 + 6.9 =$ **5.** $7.30 + 15.81 + 11 =$

6.
```
  37.5
   9.26
+   .07
```

7.
```
   4.2
  85.37
+ 11
```

8.
```
  12.7
 286
+   .03
```

9.
```
     .09
   80.1
+ 30.265
```

10. $5.74 + 8.7 + 9.6 =$ **11.** $7.30 + 15.81 + 6.4 =$

24

Decimals

Subtract the decimals below.
Place a zero to fill empty spaces as needed.

Example:

```
      5.4          5.40          5.⁴⁰
    − .17         − .17         − .17
                                5.23
```

1. 2.6
    − 1.8

2. 23.1
    − .05

3. 6.7
    − 1.6

4. 82.3
    − 1.54

5. 43.19
    − 19.7

6. 5.4 − 2.1 =

7. 6.58 − 3.2 =

8. 41 − 2.6 =

9. 17.8 − .56 =

10. 7.5 − .64 =

11. 13.9 − 1.25 =

12. 10.4
    − 2.43

13. 3.77
    − 1.2

14. 17.8
    − 11.0

15. 210.15
    − 90.87

Multiplying Numbers with Decimals

Example:

Step 1	Step 2	Step 3
Multiply.	Count the number of places (from right to left) over to the decimal point on both numbers.	Place the decimal point in the answer by starting at the right and moving the point the number of spaces you counted.

Step 1:

```
  .41
x 8.9
  369
 3280
 3649
```

Step 2:

```
.41
.9
```

3 places

Step 3:

```
  .41
x 8.9
  369
 3280
3.649
```

Multiply the following:

1.
```
  5.6
x   8
```

2.
```
 .045
x    6
```

3.
```
 6.21
x    7
```

4.
```
 62.6
x    5
```

5.
```
 2.26
x    3
```

6.
```
 31.2
x  48
```

7.
```
 .725
x  54
```

8.
```
 66.1
x 5.7
```

9.
```
 67.2
x .28
```

10.
```
 .532
x .64
```

11. .3 x 4.61 =

12. .32 x .81 =

13. 2.51 x 40 =

Dividing Numbers with Decimals

Example:

Step 1 Divide.	Step 2 Place the decimal point in the answer.	Attach zeros as needed.

Step 1
Divide.

```
        14
.06) .084
        6
       24
       24
        0
```

Step 2
Place the decimal
point in the answer.

```
        1.4
.06) .084
```

Attach zeros
as needed.

```
      5          5.6
5) 28      5) 28.0
   25         25
    3         3 0
```

Divide the following:

1. 4) .166   **2.** .4) .48   **3.** .6) 1.8   **4.** 5) .95

5. 7) 7.14   **6.** .6) .198   **7.** .9) 42.3   **8.** .6) 48.90

9. 4) 3.62   **10.** 50) 7.25   **11.** 25) 2.26   **12.** .03) .0009

27

Converting Fractions into Decimals

Step 1	Step 2
Divide the denominator into the numerator.	Round to the nearest hundredth.

$\frac{1}{3}$

$$3\overline{)1.0000} \quad .3333$$

$$\begin{array}{r} .33 \\ 3\overline{)1.00} \\ \underline{9} \\ 10 \\ \underline{9} \\ 1 \end{array}$$

Convert the following to decimals:

1. $\frac{3}{4}$ 2. $\frac{7}{12}$ 3. $\frac{1}{10}$ 4. $\frac{2}{5}$ 5. $\frac{3}{2}$

6. $\frac{1}{6}$ 7. $\frac{2}{3}$ 8. $\frac{1}{4}$ 9. $\frac{5}{4}$ 10. $\frac{7}{10}$

11. $\frac{1}{5}$ 12. $\frac{3}{8}$ 13. $\frac{7}{10}$ 14. $\frac{50}{100}$ 15. $\frac{1}{2}$

Converting Decimals into Fractions

Example:

Step 1		Step 2	Step 3
Move the decimal 2 places to the right.		Place the number over 100.	Reduce.
.40	40	$\frac{40}{100}$	$\frac{2}{5}$
1.25	125	$\frac{125}{100}$	$1\frac{1}{4}$
.5	50	$\frac{50}{100}$	$\frac{1}{2}$

Convert the following into fractions:

1. .25

2. .02

3. 1.20

4. .40

5. .15

6. .58

7. 5.10

8. .80

Math Grade 6—RBP0059

Converting Fractions into Percents

Step 1	Step 2	Step 3
Divide the denominator into the numerator.	Round to the nearest hundredth.	Move the decimal 2 places to the right and add the percent sign (%).

$\frac{1}{5}$ $5\overline{)1.0}$ with $.2$ above $.20$ 20%

Convert the following fractions into percents.

1. $\frac{3}{8}$

2. $\frac{1}{3}$

3. $\frac{4}{7}$

4. $\frac{1}{4}$

5. $\frac{2}{3}$

6. $\frac{1}{10}$

7. $\frac{2}{5}$

8. $\frac{9}{20}$

9. $\frac{3}{4}$

10. $\frac{1}{2}$

Example:

<table>
<tr><td><u>Step 1</u></td><td><u>Step 2</u></td></tr>
<tr><td>Put the percent over 100.</td><td>Reduce.</td></tr>
<tr><td>20%　　　$\frac{20}{100}$</td><td>$\frac{1}{5}$</td></tr>
</table>

Convert the following percents into fractions.

1. 5%

2. 23%

3. 10%

4. 50%

5. 75%

6. 2%

7. 40%

8. 100%

9. 25.6%

10. 3.5%

Converting Percents into Decimals

Move the decimal 2 places to the left and remove the percent sign (%).

Example: 50% = .50

Convert the following percents into decimals.

1. 90% =

2. 40% =

3. 5.1% =

4. 10% =

5. 75% =

6. 25% =

7. 54.6% =

8. 6% =

9. 15% =

10. 48.9% =

11. 8% =

12. 23% =

13. 18% =

14. 51.5% =

15. 9% =

16. 99% =

17. 5.4% =

18. 100% =

Fractions, Decimals, and Percents

Complete the chart.

Percent	Decimal	Fraction
_____	.50	_____
25%	_____	_____
_____	.18	_____
_____	_____	$\frac{1}{4}$
$33\frac{1}{3}\%$	_____	_____
_____	_____	$\frac{1}{5}$
_____	.1	_____
_____	_____	$\frac{5}{6}$
75%	_____	_____
2%	_____	_____
_____	_____	$\frac{1}{2}$
_____	.40	_____

Graphs

Use the graph to answer the questions below.

Amount of fruit sold:

Oranges

Apples

Bananas

Grapes

Kiwis

 = 5 fruit

1. How much fruit does each stand for? _____

2. How many oranges were sold? _____

3. What percent of the fruit sold was apples? _____

4. Which fruit sold the most? _____

5. Write a fraction showing the number of kiwis sold. _____

6. How much fruit was sold altogether? _____

7. How many more apples were sold than bananas? _____

8. What percent of sales was grapes? _____

Use the graph to answer the questions below.

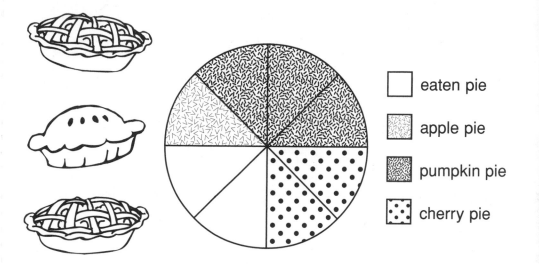

1. Which fraction shows how much pumpkin pie there is?

   $\frac{2}{8}$, $\frac{1}{4}$, $\frac{3}{8}$, $\frac{5}{8}$

2. Write a fraction for the amount of cherry pie. _____

3. Which fraction shows how much apple pie and pumpkin pie there is altogether? $\frac{3}{8}$, $\frac{4}{8}$, $\frac{1}{8}$, $\frac{5}{8}$

   What other fraction could you use to describe this? _____

4. How much more pumpkin pie is there than apple pie? _____

5. How much pie has been eaten? _____

Math Grade 6—RBP0059

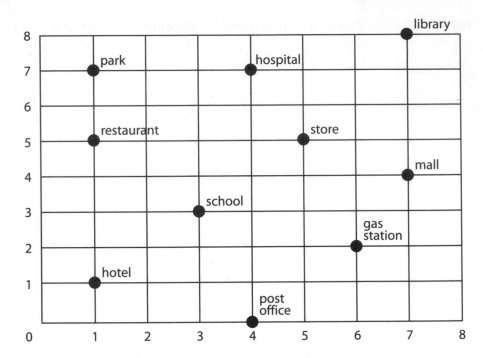

The following pairs and objects describe a point on the grid.
The number across the bottom of the graph is listed first.

Write the place.   Write the number pair.

A. (7, 4) _____   **F.** gas station _____

B. (3, 3) _____   **G.** restaurant _____

C. (1, 7) _____   **H.** hotel _____

D. (7, 8) _____   **I.** post office _____

E. (5, 5) _____   **J.** hospital _____

Order of Operations

Follow the steps below when doing problems with more than one math function. Remember to do them in the order they are listed!

1. Do the problems in parentheses ( ).
2. Multiply and divide from left to right.
3. Add and subtract from left to right.

Solve the following problems:

1. 2 x (4 + 3) x 2 =

2. 3 (5 + 1) + 3 =

3. 6 x 2 − (5 + 4) + 6 =

4. 8 x 2 + (1 x 3) − 7 =

5. 4 + 6 ÷ (10 − 8) =

6. (4 + 3) − 5 =

7. 2 x 3 − (1 + 3) =

8. 30 ÷ (4 + 1) =

9. 4 + (8 − 3) =

10. (16 ÷ 4) (3 x 2) =

Solve each equation.

$$a + b = c$$

Example:

| $x = 3 + 4$ | $3 + 4 = 7$ | $x = 7$ |

1. $y = 4 \cdot 2$ $y =$ _____

2. $x = 5 + 1$ $x =$ _____

3. $z = 6 + 6$ $z =$ _____

4. $x = 9 \div 3$ $x =$ _____

5. $y = 10 - 3$ $y =$ _____

6. $z = 4 \cdot 2 + 1$ $z =$ _____

Example:

| $2 + x = 5$ | $5 - 2 = 3$ | $x = 3$ |

7. $5 + x = 10$ $x =$ _____

8. $5 \cdot x = 10$ $x =$ _____

9. $4 - y = 1$ $y =$ _____

10. $y + 3 = 8$ $y =$ _____

11. $z - 3 = 7$ $z =$ _____

12. $2 \cdot x = 6$ $x =$ _____

13. $x + 3 = 9$ $x =$ _____

14. $x \cdot 3 = 21$ $x =$ _____

15. $y + y = 6$ $y =$ _____

16. $10 \div z = 2$ $z =$ _____

Algebra

Solve each equation.

$$a + b = c$$

Example:

$5x + 1 = 11$	$5x = 11 - 1$	$x = 2$
	$5x = 10$	
	$5x \div 5 = 10 \div 5$	

1. $2(x + 3) = 10$

x = _____

2. $2x + 1 = 9 + 2$

x = _____

3. $2(y + 3) = 12$

y = _____

4. $2x + 5 = 19$

x = _____

5. $3 = x + 1$

x = _____

6. $4x - 3 = 5$

x = _____

7. $y \cdot 2 = 12$

y = _____

8. $23 - (y + 3) = 10$

y = _____

9. $(4 + 3) \cdot x = 21$

x = _____

10. $4x = 8$

x = _____

39

Adding Like Terms

An equation is like a scale with the equal sign in the middle. You can add the like terms on each side of the equal sign.

Example:

$$3x + 4x = 5y + 2x$$
$$3x + 4x \text{ would be } 7x = 5y + 2x$$
$$\text{subtract 2x from both sides}$$
$$7x - 2x = 5y + 2x - 2x$$
$$5x = 5y$$
$$x = y$$

Combine like terms and solve.

1. $x + x + 2x + 1 + x = 11$

x = _____

2. $3 = 2x - x$

x = _____

3. $2x + 3x + 1 = 6$

x = _____

4. $2y - y + 2y = 9$

y = _____

5. $3z + 2z - 3z = 10$

z = _____

6. $3x + 2 + 1 = 12$

x = _____

Algebra

You can add, subtract, multiply, or divide on one side of an equation as long as you do the same to the other side of the equation. An equation is like a balance; if you add 20 lb. to one side, you must add 20 lb. to the other side to keep it in balance.

Example:

$$
\begin{array}{rcl}
3x + 1 & = & x + 7 \\
- x & & - x \\
\hline
2x + 1 & = & 0 + 7 \\
- 1 & & - 1 \\
\hline
2x & = & 6 \\
\end{array}
$$

$$x = 3$$

Solve the following equations:

1. $2x + 8 + x = x + 16$

x = _____

2. $3x + 1 = x + 7$

x = _____

3. $4x = 3x + 5$

x = _____

4. $4x + 2 = 3x + 9$

x = _____

5. $4x - 2x + 3 = 2x + 2x - x$

x = _____

6. $3x + 5 = x + 19$

x = _____

Solve the following equations:

1. $2(x + 3) = 9 + x$

2. $2(2x + 1) = 3x + 8$

3. $2(2x + 3) = x + 9$

4. $4 + 3x - 2x + x = x + 5$

5. $2x + x + x + 2 = x + 5$

6. $5x - 3x + 2 = x + 5$

7. $x + 3x + 3 = x + 18$

8. $2x + x = x + 8$

9. $4x + 5 = 2x + 13$

10. $2(x + 4) + x = x + 16$

In 2^4, 2 is the whole number; 4 is the exponent. To solve the problem, you multiply the whole number (in this case 2) by itself the number of times the exponent says (in this case 4).

Example:

$$2^4 = 2 \times 2 \times 2 \times 2$$

2 is multiplied 4 times $2 \times 2 \times 2 \times 2 = 16$

Solve the following:

1. 3^3 **2.** 8^2 **3.** 1^5 **4.** 6^3

5. 10^3 **6.** 7^2 **7.** 2^6 **8.** 5^2

9. 3^4 **10.** 4^3 **11.** 9^2 **12.** 2^5

Metric System

Convert the measurements below.

kilometer km 1,000m	hectometer hm 100m	dekameter dam 10m	meter m 1m	decimeter dm $\frac{1}{10}$ m	centimeter cm $\frac{1}{100}$ m	millimeter mm $\frac{1}{1000}$ m

1. 1 meter = _____ millimeters

2. 1 meter = _____ centimeters

3. 1 meter = _____ decimeters

4. 1 kilometer = _____ meters

5. 1 hectometer = _____ meters

6. 1 dekameter = _____ meters

7. 1 decimeter = _____ centimeters

8. 1 decimeter = _____ millimeters

9. 1 centimeter = _____ millimeters

10. 1 kilometer = _____ hectometers

11. 1 kilometer = _____ dekameters

12. 10 decimeters = _____ meter

13. 100 centimeters = _____ meter

14. 1,000 millimeters = _____ meter

15. 1 hectometer = _____ dekameters

16. 40 decimeters = _____ meters

17. 5,000 millimeters = _____ centimeters

18. 3 meters = _____ millimeters

19. 8 meters = _____ decimeters

20. 4 decimeters = _____ centimeters

21. 700 centimeters = _____ meters

22. 10 kilometers = _____ hectometers

23. 5 centimeters = _____ millimeters

24. 4.5 meters = _____ centimeters

Metric System

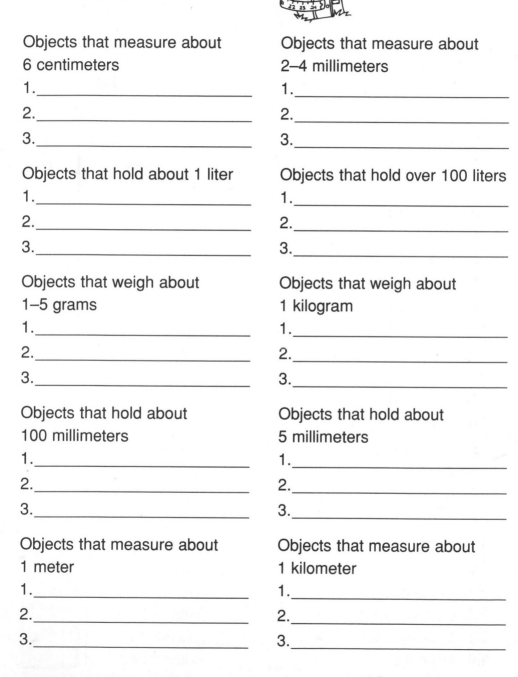

List objects that will fit into each category below.

Objects that measure about
6 centimeters
1._____
2._____
3._____

Objects that measure about
2–4 millimeters
1._____
2._____
3._____

Objects that hold about 1 liter
1._____
2._____
3._____

Objects that hold over 100 liters
1._____
2._____
3._____

Objects that weigh about
1–5 grams
1._____
2._____
3._____

Objects that weigh about
1 kilogram
1._____
2._____
3._____

Objects that hold about
100 millimeters
1._____
2._____
3._____

Objects that hold about
5 millimeters
1._____
2._____
3._____

Objects that measure about
1 meter
1._____
2._____
3._____

Objects that measure about
1 kilometer
1._____
2._____
3._____

Math Grade 6—RBP0059

Customary Measurement

Convert the measurements below.

Length

1. 1 foot = _____ inches
2. 4 feet = _____ inches
3. 1 yard = _____ feet
4. 3 yards = _____ feet
5. 1 yard = _____ inches
6. 1 mile = _____ feet
7. 9 feet = _____ yards
8. 1,760 yards = _____ mile

Weight

9. 1 pound = _____ ounces
10. 48 ounces = _____ pounds
11. 1 ton = _____ pounds
12. 8,000 pounds = _____ tons
13. 8 ounces = _____ pound

Capacity or Liquid Measure

14. 1 gallon = _____ quarts
15. 16 pints = _____ gallons
16. 1 quart = _____ ounces
17. 1 quart = _____ pints
18. 8 pints = _____ quarts
19. 1 pint = _____ ounces
20. 32 ounces = _____ pints
21. 2 quarts = _____ gallon
22. 128 ounces = _____ gallon
23. 8 quarts = _____ gallons
24. 32 pints = _____ gallons

Customary Measurement

Circle the best answer.

1. A bag of potatoes weighs about

    a. 10 ounces   b. 10 pounds   c. 10 tons

2. A baseball bat is about _____ long.

    a. 36 inches   b. 36 miles   c. 36 feet

3. A bathtub holds about

    a. 100 gallons   b. 100 pints   c. 200 ounces

4. A tube of toothpaste holds about

    a. 8 pounds   b. 8 ounces   c. 18 ounces

5. A can of soda pop is about

    a. $\frac{1}{2}$ gallon   b. $\frac{1}{2}$ quart   c. $\frac{1}{2}$ cup

6. A washing machine holds about

    a. 20 cups   b. 20 quarts   c. 20 gallons

7. A football field is about _____ long.

    a. 300 feet   b. 300 yards   c. 300 inches

8. An apple weighs about

    a. 4 tons   b. 4 ounces   c. 4 pounds

9. A giraffe weighs about

    a. 10 tons   b. 2,000 pounds   c. 2,000 ounces

Perimeter

The perimeter is the distance around the outside of a figure.
Find the perimeter of each shape.

1.

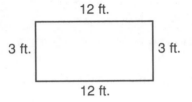

12 ft.

3 ft.   3 ft.

12 ft.

_____ ft.

2.

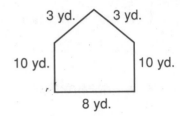

3 yd.   3 yd.

10 yd.   10 yd.

8 yd.

_____ yd.

3.

3 m

1 m

1 m

6 m   2 m

2 m

3 m

6 m

_____ m

4.

4 in.

6 in.   6 in.

4 in.

_____ in.

5.

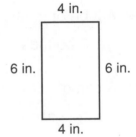

2 cm   1 cm   2 cm

2 cm   2 cm   1.5 cm   1.5 cm   2 cm   2 cm

4 cm   4 cm

9 cm

_____ cm

6.

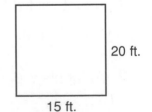

20 ft.

15 ft.

_____ ft.

48

Perimeter of Parallelograms

A parallelogram is a 4-sided figure; its opposite sides are parallel and equal.

The formula for the perimeter of a parallelogram is

$$Perimeter = 2(L + W)$$
$$L = length \quad W = width$$

Find the perimeter of each parallelogram.

1.

6 ft.

4 ft.

_____ ft.

2.

7 m

1 m

_____ m

3.

10 in.

2 in.

_____ in.

4.

5 yd.

25 yd.

_____ yd.

49

Degrees are units used to measure angles.

There are 360 degrees in a circle.

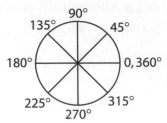

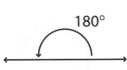

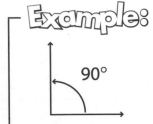 90°   135°   180°

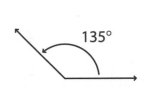

Write the number of degrees for each angle.

180°   90°   10°   45°   270°

1.

_____

2.

_____

3.

_____

4.

_____

5.

_____

Angles

Right angle: an angle that is exactly 90 degrees
Acute angle: an angle that is less than 90 degrees
Straight angle: an angle that is exactly 180 degrees
Obtuse angle: an angle that is more than 90 degrees but less than 180 degrees

Name each type of angle.

1.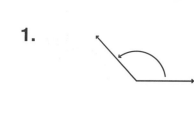

_____

2.

_____

3.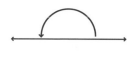

_____

4.

_____

5.

_____

6.

_____

Area of a Rectangle

Area is the space found inside a shape. You can find the area of a rectangle by multiplying the length times the width.

$$Area = L \times W$$

Express your answer in terms of square units (example: 9 in.^{2}).

Find the area of these rectangles.

1.

14 mm

2 mm

_____

2.

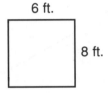

6 ft.

8 ft.

_____

3.

6 ft.

1.5 ft.

_____

4.

9 in.

2 in.

_____

Area of a square = S^2 (side times itself)
Find the area of these squares.

5.

2 ft.

6.

3 cm

7.

1.5 m

_____   _____   _____

Area of a Triangle

To find the area of a triangle, multiply $\frac{1}{2}$ base times the height. Express your answer in terms of square units.

$$\text{Area} = \frac{1}{2}(\text{B} \times \text{H})$$

Find the area of the following triangles:

1.

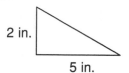

2 in.

5 in.

_____

2.

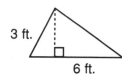

3 ft.

6 ft.

_____

3.

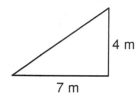

4 m

7 m

_____

4.

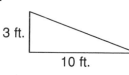

3 ft.

10 ft.

_____

5.

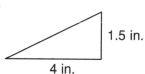

1.5 in.

4 in.

_____

6.

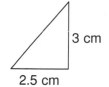

3 cm

2.5 cm

_____

7.

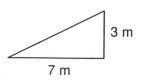

3 m

7 m

_____

8.

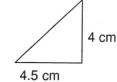

4 cm

4.5 cm

_____

9.

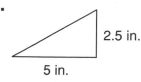

2.5 in.

5 in.

_____

Area of a Circle

To find the area of a circle, multiply the radius times the radius times 3.14. Express your answer in terms of square units.

The radius is half of the distance across a circle from the center.

$$\text{Area} = r^2 \times 3.14 \quad (\text{radius x radius x 3.14})$$

Example:

2 in.

A = (2 x 2) x 3.14
4 x 3.14 = 12.56 in.^{2}

Find the area of the following circles:

1. 3 in.

2. 2 cm

3. 10m

4. 6 ft.

5. 3.5 in.

6. 1.2 cm

Find the area.

7. r = 4 in.

8. r = 10 ft.

9. r = 5 m

10. r = 3 cm

11. r = 7 ft.

12. r = 20 m

Circumference

The circumference is the distance around a circle.

Circumference = diameter x 3.14

The diameter is the distance across a circle through the center.

 C = 3 x 3.14
C = 9.42 in.

Find the circumference of the following circles:

1. 7 m

2. 5 ft.

3. 2.5 ft.

4. 8 in.

5. 1.25 cm

6. 6 in.

7. d = 3 in.

8. d = 1.5 cm

9. d = 2 ft.

10. d = 17 m

11. d = 10 in.

12. d = 2.5 ft.

Math Grade 6—RBP0059

Volume of a Rectangular Prism

Volume measures the amount of space occupied by a 3-dimensional object. You can also think of it this way: volume measures the amount of water a container can hold.

You can find the volume of a rectangular prism by multiplying the length times the width times the height.

$$\text{Volume} = L \times W \times H$$

Find the volume of the following rectangular prisms. Express your answer in terms of cubic units (for example: 9 in.^{3}).

1.

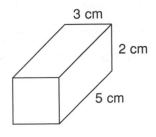

3 cm
2 cm
5 cm

_____

2.

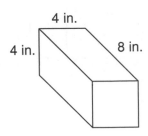

4 in.
4 in.
8 in.

_____

3.

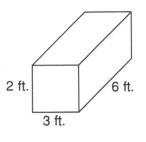

2 ft.
6 ft.
3 ft.

_____

4.

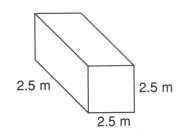

2.5 m
2.5 m
2.5 m

_____

5.

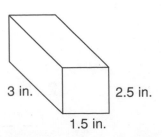

3 in.
2.5 in.
1.5 in.

_____

6.

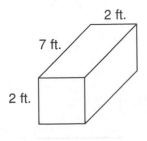

2 ft.
7 ft.
2 ft.

_____

www.summerbridgeactivities.com

Volume of a Pyramid

To find the volume of a pyramid, multiply the length times the width times the height, divided by 3. Express your answer in terms of cubic units.

$$\text{Volume of a pyramid} = \frac{L \times W \times H}{3}$$

Find the volume of the following pyramids:

1.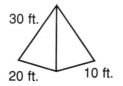
30 ft.
20 ft.   10 ft.

_____

2.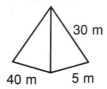
30 m
40 m   5 m

_____

3.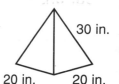
30 in.
20 in.   20 in.

_____

4.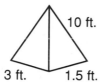
10 ft.
3 ft.   1.5 ft.

_____

5.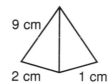
9 cm
2 cm   1 cm

_____

6.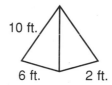
10 ft.
6 ft.   2 ft.

_____

7.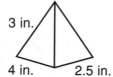
3 in.
4 in.   2.5 in.

_____

8.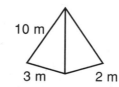
10 m
3 m   2 m

_____

9.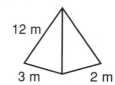
12 m
3 m   2 m

_____

Math Grade 6—RBP0059

Volume of a Cone

To find the volume of a cone, multiply 3.14 times the radius times the radius times the height, divided by 3. Express your answer in terms of cubic units.

$$\text{Volume} = \frac{3.14r^2 \times \text{height}}{3}$$

Example:

h = 4
r = 3

$$\frac{(3.14)(3)^2(4)}{3} = 37.68 \text{ cubic units}$$

Find the volume of the following cones:

1.
h = 9
r = 2

2.
h = 3
r = 3

3.
h = 3
r = 7

4.
r = 3
h = 10

5.
r = 2
h = 12

6.
r = 4
h = 6

7. r = 10 h = 3

8. r = 5 h = 3

9. r = 4 h = 6

10. r = 3 h = 5

11. r = 2 h = 6

12. r = 6 h = 3

To find the volume of a cylinder, multiply 3.14 times the radius times the radius times the height. Express your answer in terms of cubic units.

$$Volume = (3.14)(r^2)(h)$$

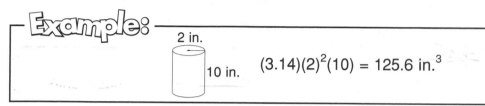

Example:

2 in.

10 in.

$$(3.14)(2)^2(10) = 125.6 \text{ in.}^3$$

Find the volume of the following cylinders:

1. r = 3 in. h = 10 in.

2. r = 6 ft. h = 11 ft.

3. r = 2 in. h = 4 in.

4. r = 5 m h = 10 m

5.

4 cm

8 cm

6.

3 in.

8 in.

7.

4 ft.

9 ft.

8.

4 ft.

6 ft.

9.

3 cm

12 cm

10.

6 in.

9 in.

Shapes

Match the following shapes with their name:

square   rectangle   trapezoid
isosceles triangle   parallelogram   octagon
pentagon   hexagon   right triangle
rhombus   equilateral triangle   scalene triangle

1.

2.

3.

octagon   *parallelogram*   *pentagon*

4.

5.

6.

rhombus   *right triangle*   *rectangle*

7.

8.

9.

trapezoid   *hexagon*   *scalene triangle*

10.

11.

12.

isosceles triangle   *square*   *equilateral triangle*

Ratio and Proportion

A ratio is a comparison of 2 numbers. The 2 numbers in the ratio are either separated with a colon (:) or written as a fraction. For example, the ratio of 2 and 5 can be written 2:5 or 2/5, and we say the ratio is 2 to 5.

A proportion is a statement of the equality of two ratios. An example of a proportion is 2/3 = 4/6.

Directions: To find the number of boys in the class, add the 2 numbers in the ratio together (for example: 2 + 1 = 3), and divide the sum (3) into the number of students in the class. The quotient is the number of girls in the class. Then multiply to find the number of boys.

The ratio is 2 boys to 1 girl.

How many boys are in a class of _____?

1. 21 ____ boys **2.** 30 ____ boys **3.** 18 ____ boys **4.** 9 ____ boys

5. 24 ____ boys **6.** 27 ____ boys **7.** 33 ____ boys **8.** 6 ____ boys

What if the ratio is 3:1 (3 boys to 1 girl)?

9. 24   **10.** 32   **11.** 16   **12.** 20

_____ boys   _____ boys   _____ boys   _____ boys

_____ girls   _____ girls   _____ girls   _____ girls

What if the ratio is 5:2 (5 boys to 2 girls)?

13. 7   **14.** 21   **15.** 35   **16.** 42

_____ boys   _____ boys   _____ boys   _____ boys

_____ girls   _____ girls   _____ girls   _____ girls

A line of symmetry divides a figure into 2 congruent (equal) halves. If you flip 1 half over the other, it will cover the other half.

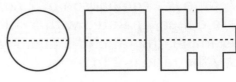

Symmetrical Shapes

Two shapes are congruent when they have the same size and shape. You can turn, flip, or slide 1 shape over the other shape and cover it.

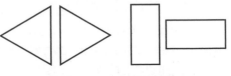

Congruent Figures

Write *symmetrical* under the figures with lines of symmetry.

1.

2.

3.

_____

_____

_____

4.

5.

6.

_____

_____

_____

Write *congruent* under each pair that is congruent.

7.

8.

9.

_____

_____

_____

10.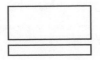

11.

12.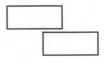

_____

_____

_____

Checkbook Balance

Mike has a difficult time balancing his checkbook, so you are going to help him. His current balance is given, and all of his transactions for the month are listed. You need to do the following:

1. Record the check number and date.
2. Record the amount of the check or deposit.
3. Subtract each check amount from the last balance.
4. Add each deposit amount to the last balance.

DEPOSITS

Date	Amount
Oct. 1	$1,450.56
Oct. 15	$1,428.49
Oct. 21	$58.42

WRITTEN CHECKS

Check #	Date	Amount
2119	10/2	$68.58
2120	10/5	$33.69
2121	10/8	$340.95
2122	10/10	$112.16
2123	10/15	$1,250.45
2124	10/18	$46.89
2125	10/21	$154.98
2126	10/25	$ 32.21
2127	10/28	$ 59.89

Current Balance: $948.56

Date	Check number	Amount of check	Amount of deposit	Balance

Ending Balance: _____

Crossword Math

Find the answer and then enter it in the puzzle.

Across

2. 6(4 + 20) + 530
6. 679 − 481
9. 8,567 − 137
10. 3,155 ÷ 5
11. 908 ÷ 4
13. 1,265 − 352
14. 1,648 − 756
15. 8,675 − 3,743

17. 10 x 64
18. 1,526 x 3
20. 3 x 9
21. 3(4,852 − 1,562)
23. 45 x 10
24. 21(5 x 5)
25. 5,000 − 1,779
26. 532 x 4

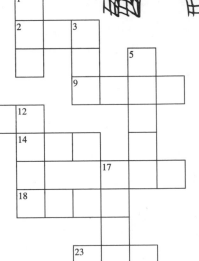

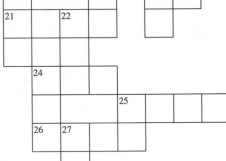

Down

1. 578 x 3 ÷ 2 − 4
3. 2,808 ÷ 6
4. 6,150 ÷ 10
5. 5,874 x 16
7. 430 ÷ 5
8. 3,487 + 3,705
11. 684 − 447
12. 3,947 x 2
15. 2(752 + 498 + 865)

16. 2,654 + 968
17. 30(352 + 2,354) − 12,628
19. 29 + 365
22. 2,130 ÷ 3 + 2
24. 1,536 ÷ 3
25. 100 − 62
27. 5 x 25

64

Spider Subtraction

Subtract the small number from the large number and write the answer in the circle between them.

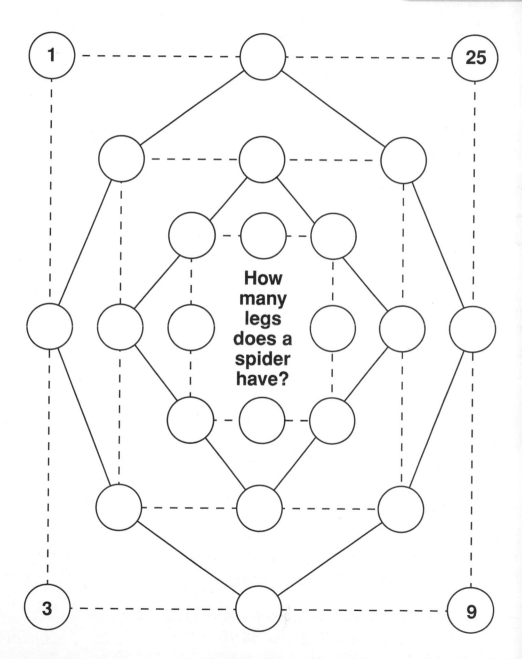

How many legs does a spider have?

Math Grade 6—RBP0059

Estimation

Estimate how much James will spend.

1. James went to the grocery store and bought milk for $2.79, bread for $1.19, juice for $3.10, and butter for $.89. About how much did James spend?_____

2. James bought cat food for $6.99, cat litter for $3.17, a cat collar for $4.89, and a cat toy for $2.38. About how much did James spend at the pet store?_____

3. At the mall James bought a shirt for $17.99, a jacket for $59.99, and a pair of pants for $29.89. About how much did he spend at the mall?_____

4. For a science project James bought a poster board for $1.19, markers for $3.89, vinegar for $1.25, baking soda for $1.89, and clay for $4.97. About how much did he spend on his science project? _____

5. James bought toothpaste for $3.99, a toothbrush for $1.89, dental floss for $4.87, a comb for $.97, a hairbrush for $2.29, and lotion for $3.39. About how much did James spend? _____

6. James went to the movies. He spent $8.00 to get in. He spent $3.89 on popcorn, $2.75 on a drink, and $2.25 on candy. About how much did it cost James to go to the movies?

_____

7. Estimate the total cost of the following: $4.89, $2.57, $6.98, $.24, $2.19, $5.78, $4.21, $1.29. _____

8. Estimate the total cost of the following: $9.99, $1.02, $4.32, $1.12, $3.78, $2.26, $7.89, $2.16. _____

Blocks of Blocks

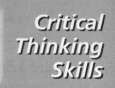

Count the blocks in each picture. There are no hidden spaces. Each block sits on another block unless shown otherwise.

1.

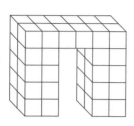

_____

2.

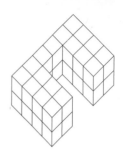

_____

3.

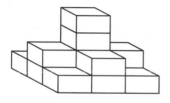

_____

4.

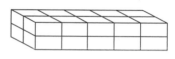

_____

5.

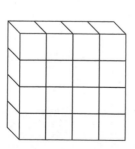

_____

6.

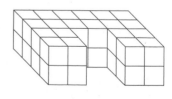

_____

Math Grade 6—RBP0059

Party Problems

Max is going to a party. Solve the problems to find out when the party is and which apartment it will be held in.

$$\begin{array}{r} 23 \\ 8 \\ + \ 3 \\ \hline \end{array}$$

1. [ ] $- 22 =$ **2.** [ ] $- 8 =$ **3.** [ ]

5. [ ] $= 2 \div$ **4.** [ ] $\times 6$

The party is at   **6.** [ ] $- 5$

7. [ ] $\times 6$ $\div 3 =$ **8.** [ ]

10. [ ] $= 80 -$ **9.** [ ] $\times 8$

In apartment   **11.** [ ] $- 17$

Pyramid Power

1. Use the numbers 1, 2, 3, 4, 5, and 6. Place each digit in one of the circles so that each side and the base add up to 9.

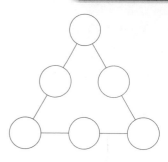

2. Rearrange for a total of 10.

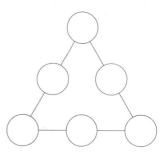

3. Rearrange for a total of 11.

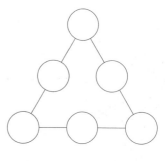

4. Rearrange for a total of 12.

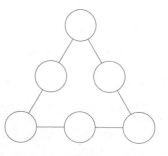

Math Grade 6—RBP0059

Word Problems

1. If 1 dozen eggs costs $.79, how much would 7 dozen eggs cost? _____

2. 18 weeks is equal to _____ days.

3. 23 quarters is equal to $ _____ .

   43

4. 24 yards it equal to _____ feet.

5. Joe has made 2 dozen egg rolls. He plans on serving 59 people. How many more egg rolls does he need to make?

   _____

6. Harry can build a fire with 6 twigs of wood. John uses 8 times as many twigs as Harry. How many twigs does John use to build a fire? _____

7. Mrs. Godina has 6 gardens. She grows 8 kinds of flowers in half of the gardens and 4 kinds of flowers in the others. How many kinds of flowers does she grow? _____

8. Myrna has 35 vases. She puts 3 flowers in each vase. How many flowers does she have? _____

Magic Balloons

Fill in the spaces on the balloons below. Use the numbers indicated. No number can be repeated. Add the numbers across each row, down each column, and along each diagonal. They should add up to the same number. What is the magic sum for each?

1. Use numbers 1 to 9.

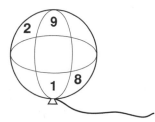

2. Use numbers 3 to 11.

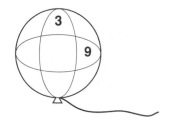

_____

_____

3. Use numbers 2 to 10.

4. Use numbers 4 to 12.

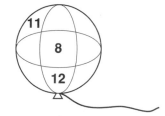

_____

_____

5. Use numbers 1 to 16.

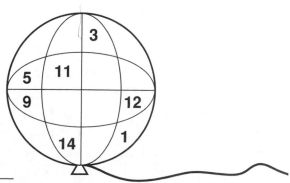

_____

Guess and Check

1. Connie has 7 coins that total $.48. What coins does Connie have?

Number of pennies _____   Number of nickels _____

Number of dimes _____   Number of quarters _____

2. It costs 20 cents to mail a postcard and 34 cents to mail a letter. Bill wrote to 11 friends and spent $3.04 on postage. How many letters and postcards did he send? _____

3. Jamie left a message for McKenzie on one of the pages of her math book. McKenzie knows that the number of pages in her book is 155. Jamie told her that the page number is a 3-digit number; one of the digits is a 4, and the total of all 3 digits in the page number is 11. On what page is the message?

_____

4. Mike drove to see a friend. When asked how many miles he drove, he said, "It is more than 150 miles; it is less than 225 miles. The number is divisible by 5, and the number is divisible by 9." How many miles did Mike drive? _____

5. A road has 6 houses in a row: Mark's, Jeanne's, Brent's, Lyndon's, Dylan's, and Alexandria's. Read the clues and label the houses correctly.

1. Mark's house is to the left of Jeanne's and Brent's houses.
2. Jeanne's and Lyndon's houses are on the 2 ends.
3. Dylan's and Brent's houses occupy the 2 center positions.
4. Alexandria's house is between Brent and Jeanne's houses.

_____ _____ _____ _____ _____ _____

Page 1
1. 115 **2.** 105 **3.** 659 **4.** 905
5. 1,576 **6.** 8,493 **7.** 8,653 **8.** 3,070
9. 11,428 **10.** 438 **11.** 895 **12.** 1,107
13. 4,808 **14.** 8,059 **15.** 4,391 **16.** 5,146

Page 2
1. 714 **2.** 4,760 **3.** 20,876 **4.** 8,900
5. 44,934 **6.** 74,529 **7.** 73,743 **8.** 10,312
9. 183 **10.** 1,547 **11.** 16,145 **12.** 13,989
13. 6,351 **14.** 6,992 **15.** 6,173 **16.** 2,135

Page 3
1. 57 **2.** 45 **3.** 916 **4.** 358
5. 403 **6.** 195 **7.** 428 **8.** 2,443
9. 7,337 **10.** 27 **11.** 485 **12.** 47
13. 3,715 **14.** 2,030 **15.** 2,685 **16.** 2,249

Page 4
1. 269 **2.** 283 **3.** 350 **4.** 459
5. 159 **6.** 199 **7.** 1,198 **8.** 1,198
9. 2,989 **10.** 6,360 **11.** 10,704 **12.** 53,936
13. 4,781 **14.** 21 **15.** 5,173 **16.** 499
17. 2,177 **18.** 67,977

Page 5
1. 24 **2.** 24 **3.** 45 **4.** 70
5. 14 **6.** 56 **7.** 48 **8.** 136
9. 132 **10.** 294 **11.** 576 **12.** 126
13. 320 **14.** 728 **15.** 1,168 **16.** 1,401
17. 2,002 **18.** 1,752 **19.** 1,772 **20.** 5,358
21. 4,650 **22.** 2,439 **23.** 1,012 **24.** 2,940
25. 2,814 **26.** 2,006

Page 6
1. 7,419 **2.** 39,108 **3.** 37,744 **4.** 3,045
5. 15,309 **6.** 14,688 **7.** 16,555 **8.** $17.98
9. $39.96 **10.** $23.97 **11.** $26.47 **12.** $28.97

Page 7
1. 20 **2.** 90 **3.** 300 **4.** 330
5. 240 **6.** 150 **7.** 240 **8.** 250
9. 240 **10.** 540 **11.** 400 **12.** 100
13.
```
 5  1  5
 2     4
10  2 20
   or
 5  1  5
 1     4
 5  4 20
```
14.
```
 2  4  8
    3  3
 6  4 24
```
15.
```
 2  3  6
    5  5
10  3 30
```

Page 8
1. 8 **2.** 4 **3.** 9 **4.** 6
5. 6 **6.** 3 **7.** 7 **8.** 4
9. 0 **10.** 4 **11.** 7 **12.** 4
13. 19 **14.** 14 **15.** 15 **16.** 14
17. 47 **18.** 9 **19.** 13 **20.** 20
21. 83 **22.** 97 **23.** 70 **24.** 656
25. 357

Page 9
1. 3 R1 **2.** 4 R1 **3.** 2 R1 **4.** 6 R3
5. 5 R2 **6.** 2 R1 **7.** 2 R6 **8.** 6 R4
9. 6 R2 **10.** 8 R1 **11.** 7 R1 **12.** 6 R3
13. 18 R1 **14.** 30 R1 **15.** 3 R2 **16.** 14 R3

Page 10
1. 18 R4 **2.** 18 R2 **3.** 6 R4
4. 12 R1 **5.** 140 R3 **6.** 137 R1
7. 94 R6 **8.** 168 R2 **9.** 267 R1
10. 65 R1 **11.** 83 **12.** 231 R1
13. 170 R3 **14.** 91 R3 **15.** 214 R1
16. 281

Page 11

Number of dollar bills	Number of friends	Dollar bills for each friend	Dollar bills left over	Write as an equation
21	4	5	1	$\frac{21}{4} = 5R1$
8	3	2	2	$\frac{8}{3} = 2R2$
10	5	2	0	$\frac{10}{5} = 2$
13	2	6	1	$\frac{13}{2} = 6R1$
18	6	3	0	$\frac{18}{6} = 3$
14	4	3	2	$\frac{14}{4} = 3R2$
26	7	3	5	$\frac{26}{7} = 3R5$
32	9	3	5	$\frac{32}{9} = 3R5$
27	5	5	2	$\frac{27}{5} = 5R2$

Page 12
1. $\frac{3}{9}$ **2.** $\frac{16}{20}$ **3.** $\frac{9}{12}$ **4.** $\frac{15}{18}$
5. $\frac{4}{6}, \frac{6}{9}, \frac{8}{12}, \frac{10}{15}, \frac{12}{18}, \frac{14}{21}, \frac{16}{24}$
6. $\frac{6}{10}, \frac{9}{15}, \frac{12}{20}, \frac{15}{25}, \frac{18}{30}, \frac{21}{35}, \frac{24}{40}$

Answers will vary.
7. $\frac{2}{4}$ **8.** $\frac{6}{16}$ **9.** $\frac{2}{24}$ **10.** $\frac{8}{14}$
11. $\frac{8}{10}$ **12.** $\frac{4}{6}$ **13.** $\frac{10}{20}$ **14.** $\frac{12}{24}$

Math Grade 6—RBP0059

Answer Pages

Page 13
Multiples of:
2 = 4, 6, 8, 10, 12, 14, 16, 18, 20, 22, 24, 26
3 = 6, 9, 12, 15, 18, 21, 24, 27, 30, 33, 36, 39
4 = 8, 12, 16, 20, 24, 28, 32, 36, 40, 44, 48
5 = 10, 15, 20, 25, 30, 35, 40, 45, 50, 55, 60

1. 6   **2.** 10   **3.** 12   **4.** 15
5. 48   **6.** 40   **7.** 72   **8.** 50

Page 14
1. 3   **2.** 10   **3.** 5   **4.** 4
5. 27   **6.** 7   **7.** 18   **8.** 3
9. 15   **10.** 5   **11.** 7   **12.** 20

Page 15
1. $2\frac{2}{3}$ **2.** $3\frac{1}{5}$ **3.** $4\frac{3}{5}$ **4.** $3\frac{9}{10}$
5. $1\frac{3}{8}$ **6.** $4\frac{1}{4}$ **7.** $3\frac{5}{8}$ **8.** $4\frac{7}{9}$
9. $4\frac{2}{7}$ **10.** $6\frac{1}{9}$ **11.** $2\frac{5}{6}$ **12.** $3\frac{1}{7}$

Page 16
1. $\frac{13}{4}$ **2.** $\frac{6}{5}$ **3.** $\frac{22}{5}$ **4.** $\frac{19}{5}$
5. $\frac{38}{7}$ **6.** $\frac{38}{8}$ **7.** $\frac{33}{8}$ **8.** $\frac{17}{5}$
9. $\frac{20}{3}$ **10.** $\frac{39}{4}$ **11.** $\frac{17}{2}$ **12.** $\frac{55}{7}$

Page 17
1. $\frac{5}{8}$ **2.** $\frac{7}{10}$ **3.** $\frac{7}{8}$ **4.** $\frac{3}{8}$
5. $\frac{5}{4}$ or $1\frac{1}{4}$ **6.** $\frac{9}{10}$

Page 18
1. $\frac{6}{10}$ or $\frac{3}{5}$ **2.** $\frac{7}{8}$ **3.** $\frac{99}{100}$
4. $\frac{7}{6}$ or $1\frac{1}{6}$ **5.** $\frac{13}{12}$ or $1\frac{1}{12}$ **6.** $\frac{11}{8}$ or $1\frac{3}{8}$
7. $5\frac{7}{8}$ **8.** $5\frac{11}{8}$ or $6\frac{3}{8}$ **9.** $7\frac{97}{100}$
10. $3\frac{7}{10}$

Page 19
1. $\frac{5}{12}$ **2.** $\frac{2}{9}$ **3.** $\frac{11}{20}$
4. $\frac{2}{10}$ or $\frac{1}{5}$ **5.** $\frac{5}{12}$ **6.** $\frac{2}{6}$ or $\frac{1}{3}$
7. $\frac{1}{4}$ **8.** $\frac{7}{10}$ **9.** $\frac{1}{6}$
10. $\frac{23}{100}$ **11.** $\frac{1}{16}$

Page 20
1. $4\frac{2}{3}$ **2.** $5\frac{3}{4}$ **3.** $7\frac{1}{8}$ **4.** $3\frac{1}{3}$
5. $7\frac{2}{3}$ **6.** $9\frac{1}{2}$ **7.** $2\frac{1}{2}$ **8.** $4\frac{4}{7}$
9. $1\frac{4}{7}$ **10.** $6\frac{5}{9}$ **11.** $6\frac{1}{5}$ **12.** $7\frac{1}{4}$

Page 21
1. $\frac{1}{10}$ **2.** $\frac{1}{10}$ **3.** $\frac{3}{7}$
4. $\frac{1}{6}$ **5.** $\frac{5}{28}$ **6.** $\frac{3}{20}$
7. $\frac{5}{56}$ **8.** $\frac{2}{5}$ **9.** $\frac{9}{100}$
10. $\frac{1}{20}$ **11.** $\frac{4}{15}$ **12.** $\frac{5}{14}$
13. $\frac{1}{12}$ **14.** $\frac{3}{100}$ **15.** $\frac{5}{16}$

Page 22
1. $12\frac{3}{8}$ **2.** $17\frac{2}{3}$
3. $24\frac{8}{15}$ **4.** $22\frac{31}{50}$
5. $8\frac{23}{32}$ **6.** $6\frac{11}{18}$
7. $11\frac{11}{24}$ **8.** $29\frac{19}{44}$
9. $10\frac{52}{63}$

Page 23
1. $\frac{12}{10}$ or $1\frac{1}{5}$ **2.** $\frac{5}{12}$ **3.** $\frac{12}{25}$
4. $\frac{10}{12}$ or $\frac{5}{6}$ **5.** $\frac{20}{24}$ or $\frac{5}{6}$ **6.** $\frac{8}{5}$ or $1\frac{3}{5}$
7. $\frac{16}{27}$ **8.** $\frac{20}{9}$ or $2\frac{2}{9}$ **9.** $\frac{35}{18}$ or $1\frac{17}{18}$
10. $\frac{40}{40}$ or 1   **11.** $\frac{10}{8}$ or $1\frac{1}{4}$

Page 24
1. 8.43   **2.** 96.17   **3.** 22.9
4. 19.53   **5.** 34.11   **6.** 46.83
7. 100.57   **8.** 298.73   **9.** 110.455
10. 24.04   **11.** 29.51

Page 25
1. .8   **2.** 23.05   **3.** 5.1   **4.** 80.76
5. 23.49   **6.** 3.3   **7.** 3.38   **8.** 38.4
9. 17.24   **10.** 6.86   **11.** 12.65   **12.** 7.97
13. 2.57   **14.** 6.8   **15.** 119.28

Page 26
1. 44.8   **2.** .27   **3.** 43.47
4. 313   **5.** 6.78   **6.** 1,497.6
7. 39.15   **8.** 376.77   **9.** 18.816
10. .34048   **11.** 1.383   **12.** .2592
13. 100.4

Page 27
1. .0415   **2.** 1.2   **3.** 3   **4.** .19
5. 1.02   **6.** .33   **7.** 47   **8.** 81.5
9. .905   **10.** .145   **11.** .0904   **12.** .03

Answer Pages

Page 28
1. .75 2. .58 3. .10 4. .40
5. 1.5 6. .17 7. .67 8. .25
9. 1.25 10. .70 11. .20 12. .38
13. .70 14. .50 15. .50

Page 29
1. $\frac{25}{100}$ or $\frac{1}{4}$ 2. $\frac{2}{100}$ or $\frac{1}{50}$ 3. $\frac{120}{100}$ or $1\frac{1}{5}$
4. $\frac{40}{100}$ or $\frac{2}{5}$ 5. $\frac{15}{100}$ or $\frac{3}{20}$ 6. $\frac{58}{100}$ or $\frac{29}{50}$
7. $\frac{510}{100}$ or $5\frac{1}{10}$ 8. $\frac{80}{100}$ or $\frac{4}{5}$

Page 30
1. 38% 2. 33% 3. 57% 4. 25%
5. 67% 6. 10% 7. 40% 8. 45%
9. 75% 10. 50%

Page 31
1. $\frac{5}{100}$ or $\frac{1}{20}$ 2. $\frac{23}{100}$ 3. $\frac{10}{100}$ or $\frac{1}{10}$
4. $\frac{50}{100}$ or $\frac{1}{2}$ 5. $\frac{75}{100}$ or $\frac{3}{4}$ 6. $\frac{2}{100}$ or $\frac{1}{50}$
7. $\frac{40}{100}$ or $\frac{2}{5}$ 8. $\frac{100}{100}$ or 1 9. $\frac{25.6}{100}$ or $\frac{32}{125}$
10. $\frac{3.5}{100}$ or $\frac{7}{200}$

Page 32
1. .90 2. .40 3. .051 4. .10
5. .75 6. .25 7. .546 8. .06
9. .15 10. .489 11. .08 12. .23
13. .18 14. .515 15. .09 16. .99
17. .054 18. 1

Page 33

Percent	Decimal	Fraction
50%	.50	$\frac{50}{100}$ or $\frac{1}{2}$
25%	.25	$\frac{25}{100}$ or $\frac{1}{4}$
18%	.18	$\frac{18}{100}$ or $\frac{9}{50}$
25%	.25	$\frac{1}{4}$
$33\frac{1}{3}$%	.333	$\frac{1}{3}$
20%	.20	$\frac{1}{5}$
10%	.1	$\frac{1}{10}$
83%	.83	$\frac{5}{6}$
75%	.75	$\frac{3}{4}$
2%	.02	$\frac{1}{50}$
50%	.50	$\frac{1}{2}$
40%	.40	$\frac{40}{100}$ or $\frac{2}{5}$

Page 34
1. 5 2. 35 3. 20%
4. Oranges 5. $\frac{1}{20}$ 6. 100
7. 5 8. 25%

Page 35
1. $\frac{3}{8}$ 2. $\frac{2}{8}$ or $\frac{1}{4}$ 3. $\frac{4}{8}$, $\frac{1}{2}$
4. 2 slices, or $\frac{1}{4}$ of a pie
5. 2 slices, or $\frac{1}{4}$ of a pie

Page 36
A. mall B. school C. park D. library
E. store F. (6, 2) G. (1, 5) H. (1, 1)
I. (4, 0) J. (4, 7)

Page 37
1. 28 2. 21 3. 9 4. 12
5. 7 6. 2 7. 2 8. 6
9. 9 10. 24

Page 38
1. $y = 8$ 2. $x = 6$ 3. $z = 12$ 4. $x = 3$
5. $y = 7$ 6. $z = 9$ 7. $x = 5$ 8. $x = 2$
9. $y = 3$ 10. $y = 5$ 11. $z = 10$ 12. $x = 3$
13. $x = 6$ 14. $x = 7$ 15. $y = 3$ 16. $z = 5$

Page 39
1. $x = 2$ 2. $x = 5$ 3. $y = 3$ 4. $x = 7$
5. $x = 2$ 6. $x = 2$ 7. $y = 6$ 8. $y = 10$
9. $x = 3$ 10. $x = 2$

Page 40
1. $x = 2$ 2. $x = 3$ 3. $x = 1$ 4. $y = 3$
5. $z = 5$ 6. $x = 3$

Page 41
1. $x = 4$ 2. $x = 3$ 3. $x = 5$ 4. $x = 7$
5. $x = 3$ 6. $x = 7$

Page 42
1. $x = 3$ 2. $x = 6$ 3. $x = 1$ 4. $x = 1$
5. $x = 1$ 6. $x = 3$ 7. $x = 5$ 8. $x = 4$
9. $x = 4$ 10. $x = 4$

Page 43
1. 27 2. 64 3. 1 4. 216
5. 1,000 6. 49 7. 64 8. 25
9. 81 10. 64 11. 81 12. 32

Math Grade 6—RBP0059

Answer Pages

Page 44
1. 1,000　**2.** 100　**3.** 10　**4.** 1,000
5. 100　**6.** 10　**7.** 10　**8.** 100
9. 10　**10.** 10　**11.** 100　**12.** 1
13. 1　**14.** 1　**15.** 10　**16.** 4
17. 500　**18.** 3,000　**19.** 80　**20.** 40
21. 7　**22.** 100　**23.** 50　**24.** 450

Page 45
Answers will vary.

Objects that measure about 6 centimeters
1. Paper cup
2. Tape dispenser
3. Crayon

Objects that measure about 2–4 millimeters
1. Pencil eraser
2. Pea
3. Shelled peanut

Objects that hold about 1 liter
1. Quart jar
2. Large glass
3. Dish soap container

Objects that hold over 100 liters
1. Bathtub
2. Water heater
3. Semi gas tank

Objects that weigh 1–5 grams
1. Gumball
2. Paper clip
3. M & M

Objects that weigh about 1 kilogram
1. A liter of pop
2. A brick
3. A bottle of ketchup

Objects that hold about 100 milliliters
1. Spoon
2. Medicine cup
3. Jar lid

Objects that hold about 5 milliliters
1. Thimble
2. Lid of a ketchup bottle
3. Eyedropper

Objects that measure about 1 meter
1. Baseball bat
2. Yardstick
3. Hurdle

Objects that measure about 1 kilometer
1. 2 laps around the track
2. 8 football fields
3. 2 city blocks

Page 46
1. 12　**2.** 48　**3.** 3　**4.** 9
5. 36　**6.** 5,280　**7.** 3　**8.** 1
9. 16　**10.** 3　**11.** 2,000　**12.** 4
13. $\frac{1}{2}$　**14.** 4　**15.** 2　**16.** 32
17. 2　**18.** 4　**19.** 16　**20.** 2
21. $\frac{1}{2}$　**22.** 1　**23.** 2　**24.** 4

Page 47
1. b　**2.** a　**3.** a　**4.** b
5. b　**6.** c　**7.** a　**8.** b
9. b

Page 48
1. 30 ft.　**2.** 34 yds.　**3.** 24 m　**4.** 20 in.
5. 33 cm　**6.** 70 ft.

Page 49
1. 20 ft.　　**2.** 16 m
3. 24 in.　　**4.** 60 yds.

Page 50
1. 45°　**2.** 270°　**3.** 10°　**4.** 90°
5. 180°

Page 51
1. obtuse angle　**2.** acute angle
3. straight angle　**4.** right angle
5. obtuse angle　**6.** acute angle

Page 52
1. 28 mm²　**2.** 48 ft.²　**3.** 9 ft.²　**4.** 18 in.²
5. 4 ft.²　**6.** 9 cm²　**7.** 2.25 m²

Page 53
1. 5 in.²　　**2.** 9 ft.²
3. 14 m²　　**4.** 15 ft.²
5. 3 in.²　　**6.** 3.75 cm²
7. 10.5 m²　　**8.** 9 cm²
9. 6.25 in.²

Page 54
1. 28.26 in.²　　**2.** 12.56 cm²
3. 314 m²　　**4.** 113.04 ft.²
5. 38.465 in.²　　**6.** 4.5216 cm²
7. 50.24 in.²　　**8.** 314 ft.²
9. 78.5 m²　　**10.** 28.26 cm²
11. 153.86 ft.²　　**12.** 1256 m²

Page 55
1. 21.98 m　**2.** 15.7 ft.　**3.** 7.85 ft.
4. 25.12 in.　**5.** 3.925 cm　**6.** 18.84 in.
7. 9.42 in.　**8.** 4.71 cm　**9.** 6.28 ft.
10. 53.38 m　**11.** 31.4 in.　**12.** 7.85 ft.